The Incredible Power Within

Padmapriya Mahendarkar

ISBN: 978-1-7370360-0-5 (Paperback)

The information given in this book should not be treated as a substitute for professional medical advice; always consult a medical practitioner. Any use of information in this book is at the reader's discretion and risk. Neither the author nor the publisher can be held responsible for any loss, claim or damage.

Book cover image "cosmos-1853491" from pixabay.com
Book design created through www.canva.com

First published by Clean Intellect Publishing 2021

This book is dedicated to

Brahma Baba, the Founder of Brahma Kumaris

Table of Contents

Each article in this book contributes to self-reflection and self-development. Reflection questions or practice are provided in the middle or at the end of each topic. You can write them in your personal journal. For any questions or queries, feel free to write to bksisterpriya@gmail.com

Positive Thinking

We sense that the world around us is becoming more negative day-by-day. In other words, the world tends to give more sorrow and discomfort to everyone. There is more anger, hatred, violence, greed and lust expressed than peace, love and joy. Positivity and benevolence have become guests in the residence of negativity.

More than the external world of negativity, we find the ongoing corruption of human minds that fuels the negativity outside. The minds run in an auto pilot mode of negative attitudes, judgments and emotions. It is as if the threads of negative energy held by human minds are weaving the world.

Can we switch back to our humanity?

Human values of kindness, love, compassion, peace and truth create positive vibes within and outside us.

Thought and Positive Thought:
A thought is an energy, which vibrates from within towards the entire atmosphere of the world. Whatever I think, the world catches it. My thoughts lead to feelings. A thought is information to my inner being.
Example: I create a thought: "This flower is beautiful" and I would feel a sense of beauty and appreciation passing through my heart.

A positive thought is an energy of information that brings benevolent positive feeling to me and others.

Example 1: I create a thought: "I was compassionate just a moment ago" and I will feel love and compassion within my being. I will feel good as I just created a positive thought about myself.
Example 2: I create a thought: "My spouse was quite helpful to me in the kitchen." I will feel loved and supported and will feel appreciation and gratitude for my spouse. This one positive thought has created good feelings for both my spouse and myself.

Positive Thinking towards Myself:
How do I create good thoughts about myself? First of all let me check what is my current thinking pattern?

Reflective activity:
1. Write an appreciation letter to yourself.

2. Form two columns and list all your goodness, strengths, talents, skills, good habits and good memories on one side and your major weaknesses on the other side.

Observe how all the negative thoughts arise while writing the weaknesses. I can think positive about myself only when I see my goodness and inner beauty.

It is a constant effort to look only at the goodness in myself. When I do this,

- I will also feel love and respect for myself.
- My expectations towards others will subside.

Examples: "I did very well today," "Wow I was really good with that assignment," "I was kind and compassionate with my colleague today," and "I value my honesty and I feel great about it."
With the power of my goodness, I can always gently work on my weaknesses.

Positive Thinking in Relationships:
I share my values and resources in my relationships and also learn from them. I understand that each individual is unique and different. Like me they also have their hero and villain characters within them. Heroic qualities are one's good qualities and villain qualities are one's negative qualities.

Relationships are where people share and have fun with their heroic qualities and accommodate the villain qualities of each other. I can appreciate and acknowledge the heroic actions of others.
Example: "My friend is sweet and gives me great company but sometimes I need to tolerate his/her temper." I tolerate not by force but with understanding. I understand that I like my friend's company. I chose this relationship and I am ok to deal with some temper here and there.

We get negative thoughts because we focus on people's weaknesses. All negative feelings of frustration, jealousy, envy and depression follow our thinking.

When I prepare myself to give what a relationship takes, focus on people's goodness and the happiest healthy memories of a relationship then I can enjoy my relationships with people. I focus my thoughts on all the good they have done for me and use patience, tolerance and forgiveness when they express their weaknesses.

Positive Thinking in Situations:
Situations can be sometimes uplifting or devastating in the cycle of life but my attitude should have the power to face any situation. I can make wrong into right, loss into profit and sorrow into happiness with my powerful attitude and thinking. Willpower is the strongest power in the universe when combined with knowledge, faith, determination and divinity.

I create positive thinking by directing my attitude towards the background lessons and hidden benefit each situation bring me.

Example: Say my company has laid me off. I shift my attitude from being judgmental and consider it as a life given opportunity for betterment. I accept that this is meant to be and perhaps I should remain free from work for a certain amount of time in my life in order to prepare myself for the next big achievement or step. I take life's tests and challenges as a father who is molding me stronger and resilient.

Hunt for the hidden message and benefit in each situation. **Example:** Sometimes one is protected from a disaster by missing a flight. One meets an old friend by getting late at a train station.

In order to understand the hidden benefit, I need to wait for time to reveal it to me. I cannot find the benefit immediately in many situations so I have to trust and let go. Wait patiently for life and time to unravel the reason.

Peace and positivity are my original nature!

Reflection:
1. In a given day, how many positive thoughts I create?
2. Let me select a relationship. What are some of my negative emotions I face in that relationship? Can I make it positive?
3. Let me give a positive attitude make-over for some of my challenging situations.

Om Shanti (I am peace)

How to have a beautiful mind?

From a scale of 1-10 defining the beauty of your mind; how much would you rate your mind?
Every human being has a mind and intellect, i.e., the ability to think (mind) and the ability to judge (intellect).

A beautiful person thinks beautifully with the balance of a beautiful mind and a humble intellect (absence of ego).

Understanding Human Mind:
What makes the mind beautiful or ugly?
Do you like your mind?
Does your mind listen to you (the being)?

Have you ever felt that:
- Your being wants something and your mind wants something else?
- Your being is seeking goodness and your mind makes you say or do the opposite stuff?

Example: Your inner being does not want to hurt your spouse; you love him/her but you end up yelling at your spouse. This is where your beautiful being differs from your troublesome mind.

Troublesome minds make situations into problems thereby giving and taking sorrow in one way or another. And this is where I make a huge mistake considering that the troublesome mind to be me (the being) and feeling awful that I am a bad person (being).

The truth is that the being is not bad but it is the mind that makes me misbehave. I can say my mind is bad but it's not always bad; it's just influenced; like the gold by iron rust.

I am different from my thoughts, words and actions but they are mine. I am different from the mind but it's "my mind." The mind belongs to me.

It is part of me just like a rusted pipe in a beautiful house. As a beautiful being I need to guide and teach my mind to come back to its beauty and give/take happiness from everything. It is a process but a beautiful process! Meditation especially Raja Yoga helps us to access our mind and transform its energy from ugly into beautiful.

A Beautiful Mind:
We all know that our minds are constantly munching on something endlessly (thinking). Each human mind has a thinking pattern (the way one thinks) and a feeling pattern (the way one feels). Our minds have been corrupted by lust, anger, greed, attachment and ego.

The Qualities of a Beautiful Mind:
- creates only beautiful thoughts like loving, peaceful and benevolent thoughts
- only sees the positive and goodness in every situation

- beauty alone is visible to the beautiful mind's eye. The beautiful mind only sees and feels the beauty of whoever comes into contact or relationship with it
- stores only nice sweet memories like people who helped, good things that happened, great actions performed, inspiring stories, spiritual knowledge, blessings, fortune and good hopes
- always dances with joy, gratitude and bliss
- never wavers and stabilizes in the sweet states of human nature like love, learning, service, inventing, offering, cooperating and sharing
- only blesses and praises; never envies or hates and never becomes jealous of any one's attainments rather blesses
- is open and generous and only sees solutions and a way out of every trouble
- never drifts from the beauty of what life offers and never fluctuates into emotions, i.e., a beautiful mind never becomes emotional rather it lives in balance with a touch of wisdom
- always stays close to God as near and dear so that God can use the beautiful being to uplift other souls in the world

How to Create a Beautiful Mind:

Believe – Accept – Love – Teach – Transform – Be
- The first step to create a beautiful mind is to believe that I am a beautiful being and I have the ability to make my mind beautiful. I know my mind is beautiful by nature.

- To accept the mischiefs, troubles, roller-coasters my mind causes me. No matter how crazy my mind drives me; I do not judge and reject it. I observe it as a mature guide and teach my mind lovingly about its goodness through meditation.
- I love my mind as it is. I do not give a hard time to myself.
- I teach my mind with the positive spiritual knowledge through Raja yoga meditation. I listen to good spiritual knowledge and teach my mind about it.
- I allow my mind to be peaceful, to tolerate and to adjust. If it fails, I patiently motivate my mind to try again. I never beat myself to become quickly great.
- I appreciate my mind as it gradually learns as I know it's a long path; I acknowledge the little baby steps successfully taken.
- I enjoy the few moments where my mind and being merge into beauty as a totally beautiful divine being. I truly enjoy myself as I am.

Reflection:

At night,

1. Did I talk to my mind today? If so, did I talk sweetly and positively?

2. What beauty did my mind exhibit today from my inner being?

3. I speak to myself "I love myself; I love every part of me."

Om Shanti (I am peace)

Peace of Mind

We often blame the mind whenever there is no peace in our life. The truth is that peace of mind is becoming difficult nowadays due to abundant information fed to the mind.

Every thought carries information. The more we see, hear, talk, touch and smell the more we think. Peace of mind is not absence of thoughts. The mind experiences peace when there is a gentle rhythmic flow of thoughts. The thoughts are channelized to flow.

Whenever there is excessive thinking about anything; the mind becomes restless and peace is lost.

What do we think about the whole day?
1. Whatever and whoever we see – Eyes
2. Whatever we hear – Ears
3. Whatever we talk – Mouth
4. Whatever we touch – Touch/Hand
5. Whatever we smell – Nose
6. Whatever we do – Actions
7. Memories – Past actions and experiences
8. Habits

Basically the sense organs outside of us bring information to our mind that causes thinking. Body and mind are very closely connected. Whenever something is felt by the body through the sense organs, the mind is the first one to be informed by the brain. The mind then creates thoughts and feelings based on the received impulse through the brain.

How to achieve peace of mind?
1. Reduce the amount of information:
In this technological world, the amount of information each of us handle is abundant. We are always seeing or hearing something that leads to some sort of thinking.

We always find something to do. Instead take few moments of pause. No texting, reading, phone calls just sit and be.

Stop all doing and just be!

Take a deep breath and feel the inner pure being living within. The more you feel your inner self, the more peaceful the mind can be. The mind is naturally peaceful but what is not allowing it to be peaceful, is the constant never ending commands we give to it.

2. The Art of Doing Nothing brings Peace to Mind.
During the day, instead of always rushing and being in the busy mode; just sitting and watching everything around quietens the mind and allows it to settle down to the inner peace.

Our worries, thoughts of actions are like the constant ripples in the pond of mind. When we stop doing and using the sense organs for few moments, the stillness of mind returns.

Method:

- Pause all your actions...

- Keep your iPhones, laptops, newspapers, magazines, all gadgets aside...

- Choose a quiet place — backyard, beach, park or a quiet corner at your home.

- Stop looking...stop using your eyes...keep it still — rest it at a point gently or just close your eyes...

- Stop hearing all the sounds...just stop listening to them...

- Tune in....feel your inner spirit...

- I am peace... I am alive... I am beautiful...I am here...

- I am relaxed...I am calm...I am peace...

3. Reduce Multitasking:

Multitasking is considered as a great talent and a time saver. It is also seen as a sign for "Smarties and Clever Heads."One's ego gets easily fed by multitasking.

But what multitasking does to your mind?

The mind gets stressed out trying to manage all our sense organs eyes, ears, hand and body in proper coordination for each of our tasks along with our brain activity.

Peace of mind is experienced where there is focus and concentration. When a single task is done peacefully with mind and brain coordination, that task is completed successfully and quickly while compared to doing three tasks at a time.

Method:
- Take a task - Focus – Do it with full interest and attention.
- Try not to think about others. Put your mind only on the current task.
- Finish the task.
- Acknowledge yourself...
- Appreciate yourself...
- Then move on to the next task...

This process will bring great peace of mind and other minds would love to be in your company as well.

Reflection:
1. Did I try some quiet time today? Was I able to transport my mind to a place of nature?
2. How much was my focus today? Write the task and its focus percentage.
3. What are some of my multi-tasking activities?

Om shanti (I am peace)

What are you thinking?

Taking the analogy of the mind as a pot, a place where we think. We think about whatever is in the pot.

Pot of Thoughts:
We create some thoughts. Some thoughts just come and go involuntarily. Churning is a process of thinking something deeply to understand it and discover a new meaning. It is done by asking a series of questions to yourself.

We all churn without realizing we are doing it. Pot is referred to the content I am churning about. Churning also means concentrated thinking.
Let's identify the types of churning as,

Pot of Dirt:
This is a pot of negative thoughts. The content in this pot is that which has created hurt, frustration, distress, fear, stress, anxiety and anger.
Example: Say your boss was unhappy with your job and the conversation didn't go well. Once you got out of your boss cabin, you start thinking what happened and get really upset with the whole situation. Each time you think about it, you are kind of stirring the pot of dirt.

We all know what happens whenever we stir dirt. Likewise, the pot of negativity creates bad smell (sadness, frustration and off-mood) in ourselves and also contaminates the environment (your irritation towards others, displeasure and long face).

We store such pots of dirt in our minds. We often take them out and start churning. Sad moments and bitter experiences lie in the pot of dirt.
Example: One of your close friends who was a business partner betrayed you. This goes in the pot of betrayal. You are unable to digest this and keep on stirring this pot again and again and share your sad story to others as well. Each time you hear about betrayal, your mind brings up your own pot of betrayal and the thinking starts; so does the emotions.

Pot of Water:
This is a very interesting pot. Lot of us like to stir this pot of waste thoughts. We invest lot of thoughts in this area of understanding life's events and others' actions. We store many pots of water inside our minds.
Example: Say you find a car has been parked taking two parking spots in a mall just close to the entrance on a Saturday evening. You get annoyed and start questioning,
- Why did that person park that way?
- Were they in right mindset?
- Why people are so careless?

So when you go back home, you again take your pot of water (this incident) and share it with your family. You may even share this to your friends next day. When you go to the same mall in a week, you remember this and again churn the pot of water.

Whenever we churn a pot of water literally, we do not get anything. It is only waste of energy. Similarly when we start thinking about such incidents in our life, we only get tired. Such occurrences need to be accepted and let gone. We could accept thinking maybe that person was in a hurry to get some medication/new driver/just did a mistake or anything positive that could calm our minds.

Pot of Milk:
This pot is our positive pure thoughts and experiences. When we churn a pot of milk, we get butter and further clarified butter. Likewise whenever we stir good aspects of our life, we get joy and happiness. Just like drinking milk gives our body strength, thinking positive makes our soul stronger.

Example: Say a colleague helped you at your work. Your kids did their homework. Your spouse made a cup of coffee for you. Your teenager was on time. All traffic lights were green that morning. You got a chance to catch the sunset. You finally finished your favorite book. Your mom made you a special dessert. You read an inspirational message in Facebook. You watched a positive video in You Tube.

There are plenty of positive things that happen to us. Let us store this in our pot of milk and keep churning about them as long as we want. Let us remember, recollect and refresh them. Using the pot of milk helps us to stay grateful and happy always.

One cool transformation that naturally happens when we are holding our pots of milk — pots of dirt and water become weaker and even disappear. Pure positive thoughts are way more powerful than negative and waste thoughts.

Pot of Honey:
This pot consists of elevated blissful thoughts. When we are churning this pot, we are beyond everything. Nothing matters. We are in a state of bliss. We are not impressed either by anyone's positive actions nor disturbed by negative actions.

We are in a neutral balance state. We will see mistakes, imbalances, injustice and flaws but it won't affect us and we will be able to take the right action at the right time. We will stand as a pillar of support and stability to everyone. Example: Elevated spiritual thoughts, experiences, deep contemplation and meditation. Continuity of spiritual practice, experience of the Higher power and expressing divinity naturally in the field of action.

Reflection:
1. Check what was I churning today?
2. Did I use pot of dirt/water/milk/honey?
3. How much time was I using each pot?
4. Which type of pot helped me today?

Om Shanti (I am peace)

Framing My Image

What is my self-image? In other words: how do I see myself?

We often tend to create our own image based on,
1. How others see us.
2. What others comment/criticize about us?
3. What others tell us, e.g., "You are useless," "You are no good," "You are not clever enough," "You can't do it."
4. How others treat us especially family and friends.

It is human nature to suspect that there is some fault in us if people around us are upset. We tend to assume stuff with people and take the blame on ourselves.

We framing a wrong version of our image that destroys our self-respect. Then we make effort to pacify the other, trying to please them to like you. All the unnecessary worry and stress had eaten our time and energy before we realize that they were not even true.

Reasons:
•   Fear of losing our image.
•   Framing our image based on dependency.

What is an image?
An image is a picture you create in your mind about yourself or anything in this world.

The mind works with images and feelings. Human beings live our lives using our sense organs. Anything you see using your eyes forms an image inside your mind.

Example: You meet a new person "Jim"; your mind creates an image about Jim and every time now you think of Jim: your mind brings back the created image of Jim.

The mind also sometimes freezes only one image of a person or a thing.

Example: If Jim is your best friend; the mind holds a smiling image of Jim. So every time you recall Jim in your conversations or thinking; that smiling image of Jim appears in your mind's TV screen.

In case Jim is the person you fear to work with; the mind holds a grumpy image of Jim.

The Secret:

So each time you are talking with Jim; you are talking with the image of Jim in your mind irrespective of whether Jim is in front of you or not. This is the reason we tend to miss someone when they are not around as we are playing with our beautiful perfect images of them created in our minds.

In reality when these beautiful images get threatened or distorted due to their behavior; we react because our expectations are not met in reality.

Example: Say you are holding a smiling face of Jim in your mind; and one fine morning Jim mad with you; you naturally get annoyed with Jim's behavior.

What's happening is: your mind wants only smiley Jim not grumpy Jim; therefore it provides resistance to reality.

The framing of images of your close ones plays a significant role in your relationships with them.
Example: A spouse may create a loving image of his/her better part when they first meet (It is said: first impression is the best impression.)

To edit this image with reality later on might become a pain as it needs immense acceptance of reality. What brings all the conflicts in relationships is to break the ego that,

"I am the creator of the image and I can't be wrong."

Creating Your Image:
It is time to check our images in our minds. We have countless images already created in our mind or subconscious mind that are of past, present and future.

The most bothering ones are the images of past- people's faces, incidents, hurts, tragedies and sad events that all together trap our current life and feelings. They block our ability to move on and create new images.

The most powerful image in the human mind is the image of the true self and that image of Higher Source. Whenever you recall this powerful image; you receive strength and spiritual power.

Something beyond image is feelings. The mind in the name of heart stores feelings too. It associates feelings with each image.

Example: Feeling of air is recorded but not necessarily an image of air.

Each image or feeling holds some power in it. It gets unleashed through a recall or remembrance. There are positive and negative, strong and weak, light and dark images in our spirit created by our own life experiences. The paint brush and the color palette is available always; the rest depends on the painter — You!

Reflection:
1. Check what is my self-image? Is it clear or blur?
2. Is it positive or weak?
3. Are they created by myself or others?
4. What are some of the aspects in my image that are influenced by others' opinions? Write them.

Om Shanti (I am peace)

Loving Myself

The more I love myself, the less I will need love from others. Do you agree? This is the eternal truth which we miss in our life. No one taught us to love ourselves. We were told to have high self-esteem, be self-confident but not much about loving the self.

What do we all seek in our relationships?
Love.

The key to experience love in relationships is to feel the love from within first. Peace, love, happiness are the most popular intangible rock stars that the whole world is dying to seek.

But the truth is they are not out there, but right within. Peace, love and happiness are discovered within. In fact "I am peace, I am love and I am happiness." I, the being of light, resonate in the frequency of peace, love and happiness based on my life's moments. Each frequency or vibration of peace, love or happiness gives me a different experience.

This is why we all prefer and seek to be peaceful, loving and happy. It is my original nature. So the entire life, we run after love trying to experience it with many people in many relationships.

We do experience it but we all realize at some point that we cannot get it from anyone continuously. Sometimes we get it and sometimes we don't. When we don't get love we fight, argue, quarrel, demand, beg, become frustrated or angry and finally get hurt.

"I love myself because I am love itself. "

All others are just trigger points for my love. When someone loves me, they are basically triggering the love within me.

How can I invoke and feel the inner love?
When,
1. I accept myself for Who I Am — no judgements.

2. I treat myself with sweetness and care — not being hard on me.
 3. I appreciate myself for all that I am and I am doing —no criticism.

4. With a lot of tenderness and gentleness I teach myself, correct myself, and tune myself — not being mean and guilty.

5. I express myself with openness and trust — not suppress myself with stress, social opinions and fear.

6. I respect myself for all my specialties, strengths and my unique flavor I add to the world — not feeling down, jealous and comparing.

7. I am clear with myself using truth and honesty — not getting confused or thinking too much.

8. I embrace my weaknesses acknowledging its presence within me but I understand "the weakness is not me". I am not going to feel awful or hate myself for that.
Just like anger is present in me but I am not anger, I am love.

When I start feeling my love, then I automatically share that love with others. All my needs and wants would disappear and I will no longer seek love but give love to all in the universe.

Reflection:
1. In a scale 1-10, how much do I love myself?
    10 - I love myself no matter what
    1 - I dislike myself.
2. How do I feel when someone I love doesn't reciprocate my love? Can I let go? Can I continue to love without expecting anything back?
3. What thoughts and actions can I do to experience self-love? Example: Appreciate myself daily.

Om Shanti (I am peace)

Free from Judgments - Right or Wrong

We often come into the crossroad of right or wrong in our lives. Things seem to be right but after few scrolling of life's pages, it turns out to be wrong.

In childhood, we are taught both right and wrong things. Parents, teachers, scholars and many other sources describe what is right and what is wrong to us. But from our own life experiences we would have noticed that there is only one absolute truth even beyond the right and wrong dimensions.

There are two angles of right and wrong.
Individual Perception:
Something which is right in one's view is completely wrong in another.

Universal Law:
Examples:
"One needs to observe silence in a library."
"One needs to be polite and humble while making a request."
There are plenty of defined laws and rules that come in the category of right and wrong.

Emotional Drama:
And usually people get angry or frustrated when the other person breaks those laws.

I need to understand what I am expecting from people is what I think is right and that may not apply for them. When I know and accept this truth then I can be a peaceful soul.

Even if they are not following the universal laws, I need to accept that it is not my duty to govern other's actions and just have good wishes for the person. If I work with people and life from an egoistic space expecting that things has to be done in my way then I am making my life stressful and unhappy.

In the verge of right or wrong, I break relationships. It takes me years of love, time and energy to create one and just one adamant point of "he/she did wrong" breaks it all.

Personal Responsibility:
I can be careful and alert myself to follow the universal laws of truth like,
"Not giving sorrow to anyone."
"Being humble when praised."
"Be polite and honest."

But let me not force them on others or react when they don't follow it. People are unique and they have their own script to play.

The Job of the Intellect:
Right or wrong is decided by the intellect. It is said when the heart works there is no right or wrong.
Example: Your best friend committed some mistake and he/she realizes it and needs your help.

In that case you would keep aside the concept of right or wrong and help her. You use the power of heart rather than the intellect. Of course you will guide him/her to be truthful but you still help her fix the mistake.

Effect of Timing:
It is not being right or wrong but doing good things at the right time.
Example: Say you are trying to communicate your exciting news when the other is in bad mood.

Any task or idea or opinion when delivered at the inappropriate moment becomes invalid.

The other person may not give her the right response because of the wrong timing. Timing of actions are important. Even though it is good, it may turn out to be wrong if done at an inappropriate time. Most of our right and wrong arguments are in our minds and it is due to our limited thinking and understanding of the people. When we become open minded and accept people for who they are and respect their ideas there are higher chances for people to realize their mistakes on their own.

Reflection:
1. Did I judge others today?
2. Do I force my opinions and perspectives on others?
3. Can I accept people as they are; beyond right and wrong?

Om Shanti (I am peace)

Am I Proving Myself?

Truth means being truthful and doesn't mean only speaking the truth and not telling any lies. Being truthful means my thoughts, decisions, words, actions, behavior, relationships are operating from the space of truth.

Inner Space:
The inner space of truth means knowing oneself and their original true self as a pure peaceful being of light.

When I think, do I think from the intoxication of my material position or inner peace?
When I speak, do I speak from the space of ego or humility?
When I act, do I act from the space of dependencies and expectations or love and respect?

Why I am not understood when I am telling the truth?
I am telling the truth but the other person cannot feel my truth until I have appropriate manners.
Example: Say I am sitting in the passenger seat in a car, I observe my family relative violated a traffic rule. I notify him/her in a rude manner.

My relative won't be able to recognize the truth even though I am telling the truth because he/she gets hurt by the manner I spoke.

When truth is conveyed, I have to take care of my manners as well.
Example: My dishonest colleague gets promoted at work and I am not.

Your colleague may have progressed forward and you seem to be backward but actually in God's heart and as per the Universal Law of Karma, you are really progressing. Sometimes falsehood and wrong ways seem to be highly rewarding and immediate results are achieved. But truly, they are deceptive and lot of negative karma is accumulated in those ways. When one is honest, he sits in God's heart. It is said: "The boat of truth may rock but never sinks."

Why I want to prove myself?
So that the other person can know that I am right.
So that I can feel better that I have made a point.

Truth is never proved. It gets proven automatically according to time. Such is the power of truth. If you prove your own truth with stubbornness, then that truth goes behind and people can only see your stubbornness.

Have you realized sometimes that when you just remain silent, the other person gets your point and realizes the truth? I need not break my head to prove myself to anyone. I am what I am. I have to just be and the truth will be visible. When I prove the truth with force, then I dissipate further away from it. Others also see only the force and not the truth. Eventually I may lose myself and get frustrated.

Why should I prove myself to others?
To get their acknowledgement and recognition.
The truth is others cannot give me that to me always. They may acknowledge one day, the next day they can reject. When I realize this, I accumulate the power of truth.
I am an embodiment of truth, spreading my rays of truth automatically wherever I go.

Reflection:
1. Do I have the habit of proving myself to others? Let me write some examples of my life.
2. Do I maintain my manners when I convey the truth? Where should I pay attention?
3. Can I spend a week without proving myself to anyone. Let me write down my observations.

Om shanti (I am peace)

Being in the Present Moment

Let us begin with a story.

Once a man was walking in a forest, suddenly he finds himself chased by a lion. So he ran for his life and stops at a well and thinks of jumping into it to save his life from the lion. When he peeps into the well, he sees a crocodile with its jaw open. Before he could decide, he slips into the well.

As he fell, he hold off a branch from a tree near the well. Now he is dangling inside the well. Soon he sees a mouse chewing his branch. Dangling there, he thinks that outside is the lion, down below is the crocodile and the branch is getting chewed by the mouse. At this moment, he observed some honey dripping near to his mouth from a beehive. He puts his tongue out and just enjoys the honey.

Understanding the story:

Lion — past

Crocodile — future

Mouse — present

Honey — joys of life

We are often chased by the memories and scars of our past and troubled by the anxieties and worries of our future. On top of it, we are constantly sorting out current issues that eat our head like the mouse.

In spite of it, being in the present moment means,

1.   To pause and look beyond the past, present and future problems.

2.   Embrace the joys of life that comes right to us.

Often we are too busy in thinking and focusing on the matters of past and future. If nothing else, the current burdens bother and blind us from the honey bottles life provides me.

So look for your honey bottles!

How to find those little joys?

Some may wonder how I find this honey drips. "I do not see them," "They are not for me," " I am not lucky," "They just don't drip for me!"

Everyone gets their honey bottles in life — the little positive good things that happen to us. They are little joys like a warm smile, a word of encouragement, someone being nice to you, having no traffic, good dinner on your plate, moonlight evening, note of appreciation, your child's hug and good workout, so on. Life offers us many pleasures, joys and happiness in many levels, degrees, ways and proportions. Our only effort is to notice them (sticking the tongue out like in the story)

- Acknowledge
- Enjoy
- Be grateful

If I am able to do this frequently in a day, then I am living in the present moment at least few times a day. Being present is to be fully aware of my being at that moment. To be aware of my inner self.

Examples:
- You feel you are in the present moment when a baby holds your finger.
- You are in the moment, when you feel the gentle breeze on your face.
- You are in the moment waiting for a score at a football game.

Present moment gives me the power to access my real self, taste my inner qualities and I feel full.

Present moment is any moment that pauses everything and gets my total attention and makes me enjoy life.

Those moments are treasures of life and whatever I do from that true space is beneficial. My thoughts, words and actions are aligned. When I wonder why did do this action in the first place, it indicates that there is no synchronizing of my inner being and outer actions.

Losing a Moment:
Any moment which makes me loose my touch with my inner self — is considered a lost moment.
Moments are lost when I am worried, afraid or basically in any negative emotion. I lose my self and that moment is lost for me. I lose touch with my base.

Formula of Happiness:

Our mind's formula for happiness is similar to running in a treadmill towards future accomplishments. It lives in an illusion of ever seeking happiness and it is unable to enjoy the sought happiness from past efforts.

Example: You had a goal to build a beautiful house. You never had time to enjoy life as you were working hard to build the house. One fine day, your beautiful house is built and ready. Now you are living in the house. First few months your mind is happy(living in the present moment) and then your mind thinks it's better to add some facilities to the house.

Again you start working hard and you forget to acknowledge the efforts and happiness you have right in front of you. Your mind has forgotten the earned happiness and started to run towards future happiness.

- Pause your life today.
- List your past efforts and achievements.
- Be proud of them and appreciate yourself.
- Be grateful
- Enjoy them as you gently make progress for your future goals.

Going Beyond:

Another meaning of being in the present moment is to let go of your worry, fear and sadness and just enjoy what is in front of you.

1.   Whatever happened is good, whatever is happening is very good and whatever is going to happen will be the best.

2.   This is a game, neither the way I play nor the result is important but whether I am enjoying my ups and downs as an observer is important.

3. I believe in my good karma and things will get figured out.

4. Go beyond the limited and see the bigger picture.

The above points will help me to let go and stop worrying.

Sherlock Homes for your Honey bottle:
At night,
1.   Write three good and positive things you liked about yourself today, e.g., "I made to work on time, I finished all my errands, I was kind with my friend today."
2.   Write three good and positive things that life brought you today, e.g., "I was given an opportunity to lead the meeting today, I enjoyed my ride home, the coffee I drank today was excellent."
3.   Write three good and positive things you liked in others today, e.g., "I liked that my spouse made my favorite dinner, I liked that my boss was appreciative of me today."

It is essential to hunt for the little positive things that happen to us. Often we forget to notice them and they get buried under our stress and worries. Let us be a Sherlock homes in own life to detect our little joys!

Om Shanti (I am peace)

Finding Balance

Balance is not being perfect and but being all right in both ups and downs of life. It is a state of being stable and unshakeable within; in other words my inner peace and inner feelings doesn't fluctuate based on external change.

Example: My self-respect is the same irrespective of whether people praise or defame me.

My self-love remains the same when I do great work or when I make a mistake. This is called being balanced within me. Balanced is not that,

- I will be always happy and nothing wrong should happen to me.
- All pieces of my life will in perfect harmony
- I will be able to divide my time and resources evenly to all parts of my life.

We all try to beat our heads to establish this sort of balance in our lives which is truly non-existent in anyone's life. Balance is being content with all the imbalances in life including the internal and external. Life is not a continuous flow of evenly distributed balanced energy. Current life in this earth has all extremes of hot and cold, good and bad, profit and loss, love and hate, peace and violence.

Being balanced in this current life is to keep myself serene and in my power irrespective of the outside chaos.

Inventing My Balanced Space:
There is a pure space within me which is so clear, wise, loving and powerful. Also there are other spaces inside like villain space, stupid space, empty space, waste space.

Being balanced means going back to my deep inner pure space no matter what space I am pushed into by the external situations and people. When I am calm, I can go inside and see what I hold in my pure space.

Pure space is where I enjoy being myself at my best.

I just love myself in that space. This pure space could be creativity, innocence, curiosity, kindness, compassion.
I am inspired when I am in this pure space.

What are the jewels hidden inside your treasure box?
Example: "I am a honest person," "I love being kind," "I enjoy gardening which indicates my nurturing quality."
Say my balanced space is like a garden where I have many beautiful variety fragrant flowers (my good space — specialties, strengths, qualities) and there are also some thorns, dry leaves, weeds (my bad space —weakness, defects, bitter memories) in my garden.

As a whole my garden looks stunning, beautiful and pure in its own way knowing the weeds and thorns are going to be cleared sooner or later. Similarly as a whole person, I am beautiful and valuable. I am enjoying being "Me" and I also progress in clearing away my weaknesses.

Being in this understanding is called Balance / Centered/Core.
- I love myself as I am.
- I respect myself.
- I am balanced.

To accept, love and respect my being as a whole including both my specialities and weaknesses. I recognize both and gently work on my negativity with the power of my positivity. I lose my inner balance whenever I judge myself and reject the negative self. To embrace and accept everything within me is being balanced.

Reflection:
1. What is my pure space? Describe in few lines.
2. Daily choose some of the positive points below to practice.
- "I am victorious. Success is my birthright"
- "I am beautiful. I am special"
- "I am a lighthouse and I give, give only give"
- "I am the support of the world. I am strong"

Om Shanti (I am peace)

Master and Child Approach to Life

In this topic, we will be discussing the following approaches to life.

1. Pure and Positive Master Approach
2. Pure and Positive Child Approach
3. Mischievous Child Approach
4. Egoistic Master Approach

First I have to choose whether I should become a master or a child in a situation. If I choose to be a master then I also have to check what type of master I am becoming. I can become a positive master or egoistic master. I can become a positive child or mischievous child. The behaviors of each approach are discussed below.

Based on our character, generally people operate in egoistic master or mischievous child. Our effort is to transform the egoistic master into a positive master and mischievous child into a positive child.

Positive Master Approach:
A pure and positive master mode is one in which I use my authority on myself — upon my thoughts, feelings, decisions and actions.

- I drive myself.
- I initiate.
- I take power.
- I communicate without expectations.

- I don't wait for something to happen.
- I take care of myself without becoming emotionally dependent on others.
- I tend to understand others more as I am able to handle myself better.
- I am mature and sensible.
- I am happy when others succeed and grow.

Positive Child Approach:

A pure and positive child mode is one in which,

- I listen and follow the flow.
- I don't think or break my head upon anything. I just follow.
- I adapt according to the group or situation.
- I am free and carry no burden.
- I use my innocence to escape negativity.
- I give in for the greater benefit.
- I do not take things personally like a smiling child.
- I easily move from one situation to other.

Mischievous Child Approach:

A disturbed child's state of mind is one in which my inner child becomes mischievous,

- The child cries in one emotion or other.
- I show tantrums.
- I become adamant that I want only this.   Example: "I want them to understand me," "I want them to listen to me."
- I become frustrated and take it out on others.

- Nothing seems to calm me down similar to a disturbed child who wanders around.
- I become restless and confused.
- I become selfish and think only about my hurt, my sorrow and my problem.
- I take my mistakes too seriously and get into guilt mode.
- I provide more excuses(not accepting anything) and point fingers.

Egoistic Master Approach:
Under egoistic master's state of mind,
- I become self-centered.
- I obsess and possess.
- I think I am right about everything and try to prove it.
- I become judgmental and less compassionate.
- I can't sincerely appreciate some one's growth or success.
- I compare myself with others and feel low.
- I want everything to happen my way and I get upset if not.
- I justify my mistakes.

We looked into four approaches, the state of minds and we behave is different in each approach.

When to use the Master mode:
- Whenever I need to accomplish something.
- In terms of my emotions and self-care.

When to use the Child mode:
- I am in a family/friends gathering.
- Team work projects.

Example: In a meeting, when you narrate your suggestion/ opinion, you become a master and share your idea with confidence and courage. Once the group decides to move on with some other idea, you become an innocent child to follow the flow of the group rather than becoming a troubled upset child or an arrogant master.

As a child, you will have the intention to stay positive and provide your cooperation for the decided idea. A child does not hold on to things. If you observe a child, one moment they cry and the next moment they laugh, forgetting that they cried a few minutes ago.

In a child mode, you can easily let go and move on to the next moment. As a master, you have the total right to voice your opinions but not necessarily all your ideas have to be accepted. So you keep this clearly in your mind that, "I am okay if things don't work my way. I can always create more ideas in my master mode."

Child Nature:
If you need to get the child's favorite doll/toy car, the child won't give it if you just ask him/her. Rather if you give the child a much more beautiful doll/toy car, the child will quickly drop the old stuff and enjoy the new one.

Similarly the mind is also like a child and is not able to drop an emotion, memory or sadness easily. Unless I trade my mind with a positive feeling, the mind cannot let go. It is stuck with the old dolls. For each of us, we need to create an emergency exit for the mind.

You create a trick that can help your mind to get diverted and not go into the shallows of sorrow. Tricks can be of some creativity that usually entertains your mind.
Example: Keep a diary of your best memories.

Using Master and Child Mode when someone is expressing their anger on me:
As an egoistic master, I will get hurt and fight back. I can hold grudges and attack the person when I get a chance.
As a weak and poor child, I can be a victim to the other person's anger, weep and wail. I can run around and complain, gossip about the situation that how cruel the other person is and how helpless I am.

As a pure and positive child, I will not take it personally and will be able to play with that situation, i.e., not taking it seriously and allowing the other person to play their script of anger. As a humble master, I hold my self-respect, remaining in my beautiful space of love, understanding and compassion. Later, when I find the other person in a calm state, I discuss the issue with gentleness and firmness.

Other situations to apply Master and Child Approach:
Situation 1:
At your work, if you are an employee, you can go to your child mode when you are with your boss and take directions from him/her.

Instead of being in master mode, the child mode will ease your interaction with the boss and the ego games will not bother you. But the moment you are out from your boss' cabin, you enter your master zone. You have all the power to handle your assignments in however way you want. You can create your own style and execution methods.

No one can stop you from being your own master.

Situation 2:
While driving, if you are in the driver's seat, you are the master. When you are in the passenger seat, you are the child. This way, you do not invade the space of the other person's actions and decisions. You will let them be and do it their way. You will not be driving the other person crazy with your driving instructions!

Situation 3:
In a family, as a parent, you can become a master and share your house rules to the children/teenagers. When your teenager/child shares his/her opinion you can become a child and genuinely listen to them.
This way your ego will not be hurt like 'I am a parent and how dare he/she can talk to me like that'. You will be able to see the point and the emotion your teenager/child is trying to convey behind their tantrums.

In all the above scenarios, we used the humble positive master approach and pure positive nature of a child. All conflicts occur because of being in the opposite zone,

- being a child when you need to be a master
- being an egoistic master when you need to be a sweet child
- being an adamant child when you need to be a wise child
- being a punishing master when you need to be an understanding one

Reflection:
1. What are my positive master qualities?

2. What are my pure and positive child qualities?

3. What are my arrogant master feelings and behaviors?

4. What are my mischievous poor child feelings and behaviors?

Om shanti (I am peace)

Being a Practical Angel

We all have heard about angels. Have we ever wondered who the real angels are! Are angels a myth or someone you can encounter in this world?

Angels are just human beings with great qualities and being ready to share them with others. In an angel's heart, there is always room for others. Angels are mindful of others' needs and understand the purpose of life is to share one's goodness with others.

There is an hidden angel inside each of us. Angelic means something pure, divine and unconditional. Such good energy is embedded inside every human being. It surfaces in certain situations and stays in the background at other times. Through awareness and silence, we can invoke the angelic energy inside us.

To believe "I am an angel" without any self-judgment is a first step towards its experience

Example:
You enjoy being kind.
You enjoy being there for others.
You enjoy inspiring everyone.

I am an Angel:
Angels come in different colors and cultures.
Find which angel you are?

Find your star angel. Trace what type of angel you are.

Types of Angels:

- Angel of Peace
- Angel of Love
- Angel of happiness
- Guardian Angel
- Forgiving Angel
- Angel of Tolerance
- Angel of Patience
- Light Angel
- Angel of Hope
- Courageous Angel
- Angel of Sweetness
- Wise Angel
- Angel of Kindness
- Flexible Angel
- Easygoing Angel
- Smart Angel
- Angel of Smile
- Angel of Coolness
- Angel of Power
- Angel of Creativity
- "Never give up"Angel

You can add to the list or choose from it.

How to find what type of angel you are?

- As you are reading the list, a quality that puts a smile on your face.
- An angel that deeply resonates with you.
- You feel content and happy whenever become that angel.

Angels and God:
Angels are always considered close to God, as God's messengers and helpers. In reality, with our higher self, each of us can connect to God directly. With our lower self (negative self) we feel quite distant from God.

When we elevate our consciousness, our greatness returns to us. We start feeling good about ourselves at this moment and just wish only give to others. If you notice, when we are happy, we wanted to share and give. That's why we celebrate birthday, wedding and success parties. The moment we become happy, we tend to smile and that is a sign of giving. You become an Angel of happiness.

The Qualifications of a Practical Angel:
Thinking:
An angel always looks at the brighter side of life. An angel cares for the bigger cause. Nothing else bothers an angel. An angel does not have the time to sit and worry.

An angel does not contemplate what others think or say about them. An angel's passion is to keep on doing his/her work as it is the service that drives the angel from within.
Example: An angel of patience is patient because his/her nature is patience. The angel is not patient for any one's sake. Her nature is patient and that's why she handles everything calmly.

Company:
An angel always considers herself to be a helper of God. We can become angels to each other and offer support to those who are in need. When our hearts are ready, God can use us. Example: Being a guardian angel is to be available for the other at their worst times. Rather than advising them, a guardian angel listens to them gently and instills faith in them.

Words:
Angels do not yell at each other. Angels always speak slow, soft and with a sweet manner. Angel's words give peace and energy to others. They make sense and soothes the heart. Angels do not jump into conclusions and believe something blindly.
When I speak considering myself to be an angel, I will be mindful to be peaceful and loving. I need not come to my human consciousness to loudly express myself.

Wings:
An angel's wings represent courage and enthusiasm that enables him/her to fly. Flying means letting go and experiencing joy, newness and lightness.
When I fly, my mind is light and easy. I easily let go and move on.

Action and Behavior:
Angels do not care for name or fame. They do not want to make an impression. They do not do tasks in order to earn a

recognition or position. Angels believe in truth and their beautiful nature of giving.

Angels glide into action and glide out once they finish. Do and Detach!

An angel's presence is gentle and not splashy like "Look at me, I am here!" "People, I have come." When they come, their presence is automatically felt and when they leave, the impact of their presence is felt. It is said: "Serve through your being just like an angel." Angels do not have expectations to be respected, regarded or worshipped. Angels receive everything because of this altruistic attitude. The law of attraction and the law of abundance applies to angels.

How can I be a practical angel?
- Be yourself.
- Find your star angel.
- Do more of what you love without any show or need.
- Keep your heart clean while giving.
- Talk to God and ask him how can you help him.
- At least a few times a day, visualize mother earth and all the beautiful souls in it. Give peace, love and courage through your mind to everyone.
- Admire and be kind to yourself, i.e., Be an angel to yourselves.

Om shanti (I am peace)

Flip Your Mood

Do you swing from happy mood into angry, agitated mood into unruffled, fiery mood into cool, amazing mood into awful? When you are in bad mood, do you feel that no matter what you do, you just can't seem to shake it off?
Well, it is time to start flipping.

Feelings, Mood and Emotions:
A feeling is an occurrence of what you feel at a present moment. Mood is a series of feelings which you feel and eventually it sets up your state of mind to a certain feeling. Example: When you start feeling irritated and then further irritated eventually you enter an upset state leading to an upset mood.
initial feel of irritation — more irritation — upset state —upset mood
In that upset mood, you will see whatever happens around you with an upset angle. You start complaining about every little issue and make your life more miserable.

Positive Example:
Say you get a Thank you card from someone, feelings of greatness and love flows in your heart setting up you to a happy mood. When you are happy, even huge mistakes doesn't seem to be a big deal. The reason is, that happiness is reducing the effect of negativity in your being. Moods are always temporary and never last for a longer period of time. There are

various moods we experience in a day. Moods usually fade off with time.

Emotion:
An emotion is a feeling that has lost its balance of energy flow and disturbs the inner state of mind. Emotion is an uncontrollable attack of feelings generated in your heart. Intellect takes a back seat when you become emotional. The physical sense organs are controlled directly by emotions. Even though you want to control, emotion takes over. Example: The reactions of your body during an episode of anxiety

Good Feelings:
Any positive feeling doesn't put me out of balance. Excitement is an emotion whereas happiness is not. Peace is my natural feeling whereas violence is an emotion.

Being Moody:
It is natural to be in different moods. But those moods have to be positive, creative, nourishing and energizing not negative, depressing, draining and de-energizing. We call a person "moody" when that one is unable to come out from their negative mood easily. The damage created by a moody person is also high and others are unable to handle their tantrums. Example: a child throwing tantrums during lunchtime

Mood hangout:
• I need to check how long I am hanging out in a certain bad mood?

- It is okay to enter a bad mood but I should be aware of how long I stay in that mood?
- Am I able to come out quickly or is it hours/days/months?

Bad moods gradually lead me to bad nature or personality. If I stay in a sarcastic mood for a longer period of time, eventually I will be developing a sarcastic personality.

Mood Checklist:
- What are my bad moods?
- What do I do when I am in a bad mood?
- What and who triggers my bad mood?
- How long I stay in a bad mood?
- List some situations that push your mood buttons.

Drill: Flipping Your Mood

For a week, practice a drill of positive mood flip.

In one second, "I am completely free"

Flip "I am a being of love"

Flip " I let go"

Flip "I am an angel of forgiveness"

Flip "I enjoy everything"

Flip "I take it easy, it's okay"

Flip "I am thankful for what I have"

Flip "I love myself — wonderful me"

Write your experiences of each flip. You can even take 3 flips, one for breakfast, flip at lunch and flip at dinner.

Om shanti (I am peace)

Smile No Matter What...

We all know a smile is contagious. We all like to see a smiling face instead of a wilted face.

How do you feel when you smile or see someone smiling?
- You feel happiness and joy.
- You are happy that the other is happy.
- A genuine smile is a proof that the other person is acknowledging you.
- When everyone is happy and smiling, you feel safe and a sense of belonging.
- You feel united and feel a connection with each one.
- Smile is the vivid expression of our innate quality.

Practice: Try to smile (a genuine light smile) at each one you see/meet today. Make eye contact and give a simple genuine smile and move on.

Types of Smiles:
- Acknowledging Smile
- Loving and caring Smile
- Happy and Joyous Smile — excitement, wonder
- Sarcastic Smile
- Dislike, Hatred and Rejection Smile — grin
- Revenge Smile
- Sadistic Smile
- Cunning Smile
- Egoistic Smile — "I am big, you are small."

- Humble Smile — "I am grateful for this opportunity... I know there are many talented people like me."
- "Take it light" Smile — while cracking jokes, fun time.
- Overwhelming Smile (when you do this, it's a sign that you are overloaded with emotions and events)
- False Colgate Smile — inner motives are different

We find all the above types of smiles in our everyday life at various venues.

How to find out these different types of smiles?
- Eyes
- Vibes

Face is said to be the index of one's mind. Eyes are the windows of the soul. When you need to find out what one's smile is about, you can look at their eyes and catch their vibrations they are transmitting. Use your heart more than the head. Make sure you are not wearing your colored glasses of perception and expectation.

Example: When you believe that the person dislikes you, then you are looking at this person with the colored glass of dislike, then even though the other person gives you a genuine smile of love you may take it as a fake smile and reject the truth.

A genuine natural smile is given always with a proper eye contact. You could feel the truth(shine) in those eyes.

Why do we stop smiling?
A smile disappears from our face the moment something enters the space of our mind.

The moment our mind starts to overthink and enters an emotional mode, the smile goes away. Smile is an external result of our inner world's status. Some people have learned the art of providing fake smiles even though their inner world is not aligned. They are accustomed to only giving fake smiles. It is as if they forgotten to smile.

Fake it Until You Make it:
Sometimes this art is necessary. We do not want to be that transparent in our lives that there is no filter. A smile balanced with composure is essential. You fake it wherever it is necessary. Not everyone has to know that you are upset. Example: A doctor has to give a gentle smile to all his/her patients even though the doctor is upset.

The doctor cannot be transparent in this aspect and look wilted as it might damage the morale of his/her patients who come to get healed. Generally at all other circumstances, it is important to be real and convey your feelings to the concerned person and not play around with false masks and illusions.

Example: If you are upset with your spouse, say it and have an open conversation rather than roaming around with a long face or a silent treatment.

If Conversations Doesn't Work:
- Stand in your power.
- Become master of your feelings (take responsibility).
- Cheer yourself up (change your mood, take things positive).
- Give a second chance.

- Forgive and let go.
- Smile and be happy.
- Give it some time.
- Let your behavior help the other person to understand your pure intentions.

Irrespective of what happens, being sad and feeling a "victim" is not the solution. Sometimes we are so delicate that even petty things can make us lose our smile. We become so dependent on others' remarks that we live like a puppet with our strings on other's hands.

My mind need not dance to the tune of everyone's comments, treatment and behavior.

How to smile no matter what?
To smile means to become master of one's emotions.
A genuine smile comes and disappears naturally. For a natural smile there is no command given to the mind to make a conscious reaction of smile on your face rather your beautiful smile just appears!

We lose this natural smile the moment we think: "That is not right," "OMG...what in the world," "Oh no! I couldn't believe they did this," "Why did they speak like that?" and "When will it work out?"

When such thoughts occur, all sort of frustrations, annoyances and confusions take their seat on the face thereby pushing my smile to the backseat.

I can smile no matter what...when I am able to hold a stable ground inside me. When I am grounded, I can accept and understand better and then I can smile naturally. The cost of a genuine smile is expensive. It is an end result of my healthy inner state of mind. I put in a lot of effort to create a healthy mind.

To smile always means I need to work on myself. I need to identify what makes me to lose my smile.

- What are my triggers?
- What are my buttons?
- What is my inner thought process when a button is pushed?
- What Am I expecting?
- What Am I resisting?

When I find answers to these questions through an inner dialogue with myself, then I can troubleshoot the exact window(reason) through which my smile flew away. I cannot smile when I cannot be positive, happy and enthusiastic at that moment. Whenever my mind loses the ability to feel positive energy and pickup negative energies my smile stops.

It is a natural phenomenon.

Positivity = Smile

Negativity = Wilt.

Therefore, in order to have a natural smile, I need to keep my inner world (heart, mind, intellect and subconscious mind) clean and clear.

Where there are pure and positive thoughts for the self and others, a smile is a natural output. There is no effort to smile, the smile will not leave my face. I will be pleasant always.

Whatever happens, there will be deep inner balance and understanding. I will see myself, others and the world with an eye of wisdom and acceptance.

Om shanti (I am peace)

Mastering Ego

Ego is a frequent visitor in our intellect. Sometimes we don't even know when ego comes or goes until my neighbor says that you had an arrogant visitor today.

What is ego?

Ego is a misinterpretation of our own self. It's like an illusion of your identity. It's part of your awareness but just dangling upside down. You are just aware of yourself in the wrong way.

How does ego work?

In the ego state, whatever idea/opinion/perception you create and you believe, that it is the only truth.

Examples of Ego: "I think and pick up a vibe that my colleague is jealous of me and I believe it to be true without verification. I am right about it."

"People tell I sing well, probably I am the best singer of the country. No one can sing as great as me!"

How to recognize your ego?

The sign of operating from ego is hurt and feeling disrespected or insulted. Whenever your belief or image is attacked by criticism, you feel insulted. That is the sign of ego. Your ego cannot accept defeat and this is why you feel upset and awful. You feel that you are always right in the space of ego.

Modes of Ego:
When my ego is hurt,
- If I get angry and aggressive, I am in superior complex mode.

- If I get sad and feel low, I am in inferior complex mode.

All the suffering and sadness is due to the misunderstanding of the self, others and life. My Ego tricks me to look at something else; it drifts me from reality and blurs my vision. In ego, I assume whatever I think, decide and act is right and others are quite wrong.

This perception of mine makes me miserable as I constantly find how much others are wrong and how oddly they do not agree with me that I am right. I fight, fight and fight in proving myself. I get caught up in this continuous frustration. Then I label them as 'bad people' and give them hard time whenever I get the chance. If they are too powerful, I wine, weep and gossip!

Realizing and Treating Ego:
I needs to step back to understand that it is my ego that is operating me. Most times I don't realize on what basis I am thinking or looking at things. It happens so subconsciously that I don't even realize my own arrogance whereas others can see it clearly.

Meditation enables me to observe myself frequently. When I am observing myself, I observe my actions, related thoughts and feelings, leading perceptions, hidden beliefs and finally the behind-the-curtain space of ego. To identify the ego, truth is essential. I need to understand that, "I am not what others think" and "what others think about me is not making my life."

All the false learned and ancestry beliefs sustain my ego; my false image. Ego is learned since childhood. The more I realize the truth, the ego lessons.

Truth always forgives the mistakes of others whereas Ego does not forgive others that easily. Ego says they deserve punishment. Truth says they deserve compassion.

Example: Ego says: "I have the best house in this whole city." Truth or Self-respect says: "I have the best house and there are many other great houses in the city as well."

When I understand both the spaces of ego and truth within me, it is easy to ascertain:
- when I am using my ego
- at what circumstances
- how I can switch to my truth

Excuses for Ego:
We do give excuses to justify our ego. In ego, our judgment becomes partial and biased. Ego never accepts that it has made a wrong judgment. Ego never accepts its fault. Anything done from the space of ego is overly protected and when it is challenged, I become defensive.
Example: My ego is the one which makes me tell ten lies to cover one lie. Why? Because I am unable to accept that I am a

liar and there is fear of losing my image. Under the space of ego, I feel whatever I do is right. I will give many excuses justifying my need for committing a wrong action.

Becoming Ego Free:
Self-respect, Humility and Honesty are the divergent spaces of Ego. When I am in this positive space, I can easily accept my mistakes and show interest to learn and change.

1. Spending quality time with my inner being daily. Speaking to myself positively.

2. Creating a positive image about myself and believing in it with an attitude of improvement.

3. Respecting myself and others for who they are including their defects, mistakes and personality.

4. Appreciating my uniqueness, specialty, talent, attainments. I also value the same of others. I delete this egoistic belief "I am the only one."

Right from childhood, we have been taught to compete and become number one. That means I should be UP even if it means to put everyone down. We are educated and applauded to beat everyone up. This is the wrong benchmark of success. This attitude only nurtures my ego and makes me insecure when others go forward.

True Success is to master and grow one's own abilities and skills keeping others as markers and references in that process not rivals and enemies. We learn from each other and my goal is not to defeat them.

Truth says I become number one and I also inspire others to become number one or the best they can. I respect everyone and I do not prove myself to show how smart I am. I understand that everyone is great in their own way.

5. Listening to corrections and advises of others without proving myself. I know myself and I need not make it a point for others to agree.

6. Loving my entire being as it is. Appreciating my strengths and patiently working on my weaknesses.

7. Apologizing for my weaknesses without losing my self-respect. To understand it's okay for everyone including me to make mistakes as no one is perfect in this world. I will do my best to be cautious and not hurt anyone.

Where there is self-realization, ego disappears.

Om shanti (I am peace)

Are you in your comfort zone?

All of us live in our comfort zones without realizing that they are zones or spaces created by us to comfort us.

Comfort zone is like a pillow in your sofa. When taken out, you feel the emptiness or the difference. Consciously or unconsciously we all have created such pillows.

Zooming into Comfort Zone:
Comfort zones are those materials, habits, people and places which we are accustomed to.
Example your coffee mug
You use your coffee mug daily and one day if it's missing, you feel the difference. Your heart runs to your coffee mug again and again. That is your comfort zone.

Some of the examples of your comfort zone:
Your regular gas station.
Your routine walk route or route to your work/home.
Your seat preference in a flight.
Your usage of phone like WhatsApp or texting.
Your home and your favorite TV Shows/Sport channel.

You feel discomfort whenever there is any change like a detour from your usual route. The moment you find the detour sign, your mind tells "Oh no, now I need to figure out another route!". This is where you are pushed to come out of your comfort zone by life. You can end up having a new experience or amplify the route with your laments.

Why can't I come out of my comfort zone?
I am habitual in my comfort zone as I have trained myself to be in there. I do not train consciously, but it happens. Only when life snatches it away or I am compelled to leave it, I realize that it was my comfort zone.

Comfort zone is a feeling of being home and safe just like sleeping in my own bed. It is difficult for me to let go and exit my comfort zone because I am attached to this safety and easiness of being home. I do not want to leave this homey feeling forever. It is like kids refusing to go to the first day of school. Home is the kid's comfort zone but until the kid leaves it behind, the kid can't progress.

Eating junk food is a comfort zone but until I leave it and enter a zone of proper diet and exercise, there is no result. Similarly changing jobs, moving to a new city, entering new relationships is all about stepping out of my comfort zones and entering a new zone. I could also make the new zone as a comfort zone by simply attaching to it and refusing to let go of it.

Even emotions like fear, anger, sadness and habits of low self-worth, complaining and gossiping are comfort zones. The being is so comfortable in gossiping that it likes doing it, even enjoys it and never feels an effort to gossip. Whereas to stop gossiping is an effort. The being has to come out of the habit of gossiping(stepping out of comfort zone) and create new practice of appreciation.

What happens when I come out of my comfort zone?
I have to use my brain again to think and rediscover new strategies, ideas and solutions.

It is an effort to take my mind towards acceptance and flexibility. And this is why I do not want to exit my comfort zone.

I would like to hang around and try hard to go back to my comfort zones. I deny change and call it as unfair. When I exit momentarily and go back to my comfort zone, I resume my joy. The reason for that joy is I have just saved myself from the effort of reprogramming my mind and intellect. I have saved emotions of loss and grief. This is why I feel happy when I find back the lost.

External matters are just a trigger, prominence goes to the inner work. But escaping the inner work doesn't help in the long run. One day or other, I need to face the reality of stepping out of my comfort zone.

Ways of stepping out of your comfort zones:
1. Try a different route to your work/home.

2. Visit another gas station or restaurant.

3. Try Tech-Fast (no iPhone, laptop, TV for a day)

4. Meet a new friend. Eat lunch with someone you usually don't.

5. Change things around in your house. Move around your sofa/bed to different corners. Donate stuff to the needy.

6. Cook a new dish.

Reflection:
When you play around shifting things outside, things shift inside too.

- Observe how many strings you are attached to.
- What was difficult for you to let go and adapt?
- What was easy for you to change?
- What did you enjoy?
- Did you experience newness and learn something?

Om shanti (I am peace)

The Habit of Speaking Unnecessary Lies

We sometimes develop the habit of telling unnecessary lies. This habit lurks so much in the background that we fail to realize how many unnecessary lies we utter for our convenience.

Why do we lie?
- To preserve one's dignity.
- To save from embarrassment.
- Not to lose one's image in front of a person or family/friends group.
- Image in the society.

If you observe, the situations where we speak unnecessary lies are only petty ones. But the habit gets stoned in the self. We just lie even without bothering about it. We want to make a nice opinion or image about our self towards the other person. The second we utter that lie, our consciousness bites. We just ignore that bite assuring ourselves that it's not a big deal. Example: When you forget something repeatedly, you lie to make it up. You consider yourself to be hardworking and usually do not make mistakes but when you do, you lie to keep up that hardworking person image.

In order to please the other person, you lie that they look great today but you don't mean it. All these unnecessary lies do create a waste atmosphere and decreases your percentage of authenticity about yourself.

It's not only a matter of someone catching you make the unnecessary lie but this negative habit is being developed unconsciously in yourself.

How can you stop telling unnecessary lies?
Awareness and Strong decision:
When I create a liking to be clear and honest, I can make a decision not to utter any lies even for petty reasons. I will observe myself and keep guard.

Being mindful of my words:
When I become mindful of my words and presentation, I can easily avoid unnecessary lies.

Admission of my mistakes and flaws:
It's all right for me to allow my image to slightly glide down in front of the other person. I know no one is perfect in this world. If I admit my little mistakes and flaws, I will get no reason to lie.

Letting Go of what Others will Think of Me:
I can tell myself that it's not a big deal if people think that is a foolish mistake. It will not make me a fool if people think that I am a fool. It just their judgment of looking at my one wrong action. No one sees me 360 degrees therefore no one can truly judge me.

I need not feel bad:
Even if something happens, instead of trying to make up the situation by telling unnecessary lies, I can better tell the truth.

At least I can feel good about being honest.

Reflection:
Let me reflect,
- Did I say any unnecessary lies today?
- What was the reason for me to lie?
- Can I manage the situation without speaking lies?

White Lies:
White lies are a whole another topic. White lies are lies told for a benefit. There is no hidden or selfish motive in white lies. It is told for the overall benefit of others and the world. White lies can be called as tactics (intelligent alternative), confidential, restricted, top secret, sensitive and nonpublic information.
Examples:
- A doctor saying to the patient who just had a heart attack that he is doing great even though he is not.

- On an important day at your spouse's workplace, you hide your sickness so that your spouse's mind can be free for his/her important day.

- You know the tantrum your kid will exhibit when his toy is destroyed, so you replace the kid's favorite toy quietly.

Why white lies are used?
- In order to protect others
- Avoid unnecessary drama
- Emotional condition of others

- Personality history of others
- Confidentiality

Not everything needs to be revealed to the whole world. Information can be moderated according to the person and time.
Example: At work, the management carry confidential information that cannot be shared with all employees. It is not called a lie when they don't share it.

The mindset, timing and the heart level of the other person has to be considered before we share certain information.

Some matters needs to be accommodated within the self or a small group. Certain things can have a work around instead of telling the exact truth and damaging the heart of the other. It's purely based on the specific circumstance. I also need to be aware of using white lies for selfishness. Having discussed all this doesn't give us a passport to continue to speak white lies for every little incident.

White lies need to be used only in absolutely necessary conditions. They are like emergency kits and not for daily use. If you do, it won't be a white lie anymore, it will just be a lie!

Om shanti (I am peace)

The Art of Doing Nothing

When we hear the word "nothing," it is easily interpreted as idling and waste of time. But 'the nothing space' is the true space every meditator seeks within.

"Nothingness" is a state of fullness. It is the space inside you which enables you to create or give your best. It is like a plain canvas where anything can be painted.

Can your mind be a plain canvas? A blank space?
Art of doing nothing is an art of settling one's mind into this space of nothing/stillness like a plain canvas. Often, the word 'nothing' is misinterpreted and judged in terms of doing, i.e., action.

We are called human "beings" not human "doings."

We do from the space of a being, i.e., action arises from within. And now, we are all more into doing and less in being. "Being" is forgotten under the initiation, action and result of "Doing" to the extent that we consider our "Being" to be something that we are "doing."
Example: I am a dancer, I am an architect.
My profession is dance or architect but my being is not my profession. I, the being is enabling my body to perform actions. Profession is just one of the many actions my being executes.

Because of this misunderstanding, instead of feeling our true being which is full of peace and happiness, we feel sad as we depend our feelings on "doing." It is as if the tail has become the head and we move in the wrong direction.

Art of doing nothing enables you to see your inner source and value it. When you are made to sit and do nothing for days, you will eventually lose your self-worth. Because the input (action to being) is zero, the respect generated also becomes zero. But when you learn the art of doing nothing, even though you are just sitting and literally doing nothing, there is a sense of contentment and self-respect for the "being" which is radiating and expressing itself through the beautiful thoughts and feelings.

When you experience the presence of your inner being in that state of nothingness that is completely beyond the pull of actions or the urge to do constantly something, then the mind becomes a plain canvas. Like the pond settles down to stillness, new ideas arise. Solutions emerge.

There is a clear direction to perform an action with the deep feeling of the "being" initiating that action rather than the constant stressful flow of doing actions.

There is no clue of what's going inside and only undergoing emotional roller-coaster as you do, do and do. Actions that are done with the awareness of "I, the being" create more impact.

What is the "Being"?

"Being" is where I think, feel and a space where all my true qualities exist.

Ask yourself,

1. What are the actions that really spark your "being" up? In other words, what actions moves your inner being?

2. Describe your inner being. What is that little inner positive voice telling you?

3. List all your specialties, strengths and good aspects which you admire about yourself (at least ten).

The art of doing nothing makes you "be"more and to emerge from that: "being" towards "doing."

Nurturing your being:

There are actions we have to do as part of our duties and responsibilities. But how often we act from the core of our being? What actions arise from our inner specialties?

Example: If you love singing, do you give some time and nurture it or you just suppress it? Basically the heart guides you to do what you love. And that love has no agenda.

Example: If you, the being is creative, your heart would love to do creative work like painting, singing, dancing, writing, handicrafts.

You may not nurture this part of your being as you get lost into your daily role of being a parent/employee. This leads to some sort of inner emptiness which pops up as discontent, stress, sadness.

We nurtured our hobbies and things we loved to do when we were kids. And that's why kids are happier than the adults as they feel the "being" more in the "doing." As we grow, we give importance to "doing" that is necessary and profitable and we miss our "core" being that needs attention as well.

Reflective Activity:
Every week, do something that reflects most of your "being."
1. Follow up on a hobby which you stopped doing. Feel your "being."
2. Another method to feel your core is to be in meditation.

Raja yoga meditation pulls you off from actions, illusions of the mind and connects to your inner being and gently releases back to your life of doing. Meditation is an art of refreshment and the power of "nothingness" thus evolves.

Om Shanti (I am peace)

The Art of Saying "No"

Some of us find it very difficult to say, "No" to people. To say, "No" to someone is so hard that we just say, "Yes" to things we can't do or do not want to do.

Why do we say, "Yes" instead of "No"?
- We want to please the other person.
- We do not want to let down our image "I am very nice," "I am always helpful and supportive."
  Example: You are habitual in helping others in need. Then subtly there is an ego created that, "I am kind and I am supposed to help no matter what." Slowly instead of kindness, it becomes an obligation (inside your head) for you to help.
- Fear of other consequences.
  Example: When we say, "No" to people who are in higher position than us like a boss/parent, then there is a fear of consequence.
- We feel we could handle it all.
- Fear of rejection by the other person.
- We are too kind that we just can't say "No"
- We do not want to hurt the other person.
- We just can't bear to see that "sad" face after we say, "No." In other words we do not want to disappoint others.
- We just don't want to handle the tantrum of the other person.
  Example: Most parents just hand over whatever the

kid demands because they do not want to handle the tantrum the kid throws after saying No.

Repercussion of saying Yes instead of No:
Since I have said, "Yes" to things that I cannot do or manage, the following drama happens to the self and others in the process.

Self:

- I feel pressured because I have to do it now as I have given my word.
- Things get delayed as I have too much on my plate. I am overloaded.
- I procrastinate.
- I get overwhelmed with many tasks, projects, and activities I have committed to.
- I have created an unsaid expectation for others as I have said,"Yes." Now I have to fulfill that expectation.
- I tend to do things at the last minute because I have too many things to handle. Therefore I do not take action until the time comes. I do not get a chance to prepare myself sufficiently.
- I do not plan either because it's too much to cope with if the plan changes.
- I put myself in peak stress like rushing, making others wait, ignoring the phone calls, incomplete finish. Overall I perform a poor job.
- I also provide false assurances to the person so that they could feel I'm working on that task (whereas I'm really unable to). It's not my intention but I do not have the courage to say, "Sorry, I can't do it. I'm busy."

- I compromise on the quality of the product or service I am offering.
- I really want to help this person and it is an important relationship for me but I am also overburdened with other responsibilities. So I play the "Yes" game on both ends and get into trouble on both sides.

Example: A husband promising his wife to take her for dinner on their wedding anniversary. The wife initiated the dinner invitation and the husband says, "Yes" in spite of his conflicting task on the same date. He says, "Yes" to please his wife as he really loves her and wants to keep her happy too.

At the same time, at his workplace, his boss has already scheduled him to an important meeting. He is caught up between work and family. He is unable to speak up and say, "No" to either side.

The he makes his wife wait at the restaurant by telling her that he is on his way while he was still in the meeting. You know what happens when the wife finds out. But if he has learned the art of saying, "No" to either his boss or to his wife, he could have saved himself the tension and also the disappointment of others.

Others:
- They get upset with you, as you couldn't keep your word.
- If your committed task gets delayed, they might lose their trust in you.

- You lose your integrity when you over-commit yourself.
- People count on you and when you delay, it is not fair to them. They could see that you are overloaded but they have no choice as they have booked you for that task. You give them no choice but to follow-up with you. Karmically this is not good karma either as the person is being stressed out due to your lack of attention and commitment.
- It is rather better to say, "No" and not do the task than saying, "Yes"and not doing the task.
- It is not fair to make someone wait, to waste the time of others, to stress others when you know they are depending on you, to prolong them and try to buy their trust.

You can have a kind, compassionate heart but at the same time to understand your capacity and committing accordingly is also important.

How to say "No"
We do say, "No" but the way we say it is blunt and when you see the consequences of your blunt "No" you will hesitate to say, "No" next time.

The manner we say, "No" is very important. The tone, body language and the audacity of saying, "No" play an important role in not hurting the other person. When someone is hurt, especially when their ego or identity is hurt, they can revenge with you. Half the crime in the world happens just because some one's ego is hurt.

Example: If you say, "No" in a harsh manner to your manager for an assignment, you are likely to earn his revenge like he may block your opportunities or even fire you.

Sometimes we say, "No" with a frustration or a blunt harsh tone.

The proper manner to say, "No"

Instead of directly saying, "No" you can say, "I would be happy to do it but...," "I would love to help you but...," "I wish I could do it for you but...," "I am very sorry." People like to hear a yes first then their heart is prepared for your "No"otherwise micro heart attacks(hurt) happen. People get irritated or upset when they hear an immediate "No."

- They will understand when you explain your scenario and express a sincere interest in helping them.
- A lot of them tend to say, "No" flat onto someone's face, which offends the requesting person. You may be in a doomsday hurry but the other person may not realize it. That is why it's extremely important to be kind and polite even under stressful circumstances.

Think: How will you answer your kid who is asking you to get him a video game when you are getting ready to leave to work on a Monday morning? You can just say a blunt "No" or even yell at your kid and leave to work. But this rude behavior will hurt your kid and also bother your conscience.

How to say a polite 'No' in this situation:
"Let's think about it dear!" "Sure, let's talk about it in the evening...now enjoy your school." You can also add some loving words. This manner of speaking will give a positive acknowledgment to your kid that his father or mother cares for him/her always. You can have a conversation or say, "No" with an explanation when you go back home.

Just because someone catches you at the wrong timing, it doesn't give you a permission to act rude.

You need to cultivate the art of expressing yourself peacefully at the same time firmly at critical and stressful moments. This comes with:
- self-realization
- a kind way of self-monitoring
- gentle reminders of attention and practice

It is an act of integrity when you keep your word. When you say five minutes you really mean five minutes. Those who can't say, "No" are forced to tell lies, compromise, be late and juggle many things at a time. When you say five minutes, if it takes one hour as you are doing many things in one hour, then others lose trust in you. You can possibly lose your integrity and respect. They may respect you for your generous kind heart but will not respect your inefficiency and non-commitment.

Reflection:

- Observe – In a day how many activities do I end up doing just because I gave a commitment to the other person?

- How many tasks do I not complete on time? (because I couldn't say no)

- What were my past consequences when I couldn't keep my word? Can I fix it? Can I heal those relationships by sincerely saying, "Yes" when I can and "No"when I can't?

Om shanti (I am peace)

Sensitivity and Sensibility

We all become sensitive of something in our life. Sensitivity is to sense what is going on and Sensibility is how I respond after I have sensed. Being emotionally sensitive is like sensing a presence of an emotion, feeling, attitude, intention and the vibe of the other person or an environment.

Example: I am sensitive to all hidden ways of rejection like eye contact, body language or even just the vibrations. I pick up them quickly without any physical signs from the other person. I am sensitive to the gossip environment. I pick up the heavy energy of sadness in the air.

Being sensible is to act from the space of clarity and understanding.

Example: Knowing all the games of the gossip environment, I act clever and kind. I keep myself clear and express good wishes of my heart.

One is to be sensitive and the other is being sensible.

What to do when you are sensitive?
Whenever I sense something, say I pick up the energy of some of my colleagues are against me at my workspace. The moment I pick this up, I become judgmental about it and react to that picked up sense or vibration. I may become cranky and rude to my colleagues.

Just like our nose picks up some smell or fragrance and gives us an input and then it's up to our brain to use it or ignore it. Likewise understanding that I am a master of my senses including my emotional senses.

1. I separate myself from it.

2. I use my sensibility — understanding, knowledge, experience in the situation.

3. I act accordingly — take it positive/just ignore/correct whatever is wrong on my side.

Feeding on to it and feeling awful is like self-sabotaging myself. It is as if my own hand is attacking me. I allow my emotional sense to make my being confused and doubtful. Being sensible is to be smart in protecting my inner peace. It is clever not to get carried away by all the things I pick up even though some of it might be true.

Causes of Sensitivity:
Another reason for sensitivity is fear of people's opinion and a background expectation that each one should like me and understand me. Spirituality teaches me to be free from the world's opinion and give power to my own thinking.
Also no matter how best I do, there always shall be a few people who will find fault.

Sensibility is to understand that I never have the need to prove myself and secure myself.

Whatever is meant for me will come to me and there are lots of good karma out there which I invested finding their way back to me! My inner beauty always shines and I take care that I do not allow the dust of picking waste useless negative energy of others or environment to hide my sparkle.

Om shanti(I am peace)

Human being's Intention Vs Behavior

There are two parts of an action. There is presentation of an action and the intention behind that action.

Example: A person in a billing counter having a kind intention will help his customers with love and a smile (presentation of kindness)

Here both the intention and presentation of that intention is good. Both the giving and receiving person are happy. The intention and presentation can categorize people in the following groups.

Category 1:

There are some people whose intentions are good but the way they present their intention in action is poor. They present in such a way that the other person gets hurt and do not see their intention (where they are coming from).

Example: Parents have pure and good intention for their children, but when they come into action for correction; their presentation is of yelling, anger and force. Love is not seen in their words or actions even though their heart is full of love and benefit.

Consequence: When the presentation or behavior is hurtful and negative, both the parties suffer. The A party in this category feel that they are doing right and for a right cause but the B party do not understand their heart. The presentation highlights the emotions thereby others fail to see the good intention.

Both parties get hurt and there is no harmony in their relationship.

Action Required:

One needs to understand the effect of their behavior on others and work on developing a sweet, pleasant, cool and kind mannerism.

Category 2:

The souls of this category are interesting. Their intentions are not very pure but their presentation is great. So they get along easily with everyone. People love such category souls. You may notice such souls in your work or family environment. Even though their intentions are not very clean, because of sweet words, smiles and loving actions, they become temporarily successful. Everyone gets impressed with such behavior.

A fairytale example: The stepmother of Snow White disguises herself as an old woman and the way she tempts Snow White to consume that apple was so kind and sweet that Snow White couldn't resist it.

It is not to label that people are bad or evil; No. We all fall under this category when we perform actions like that. This category of souls have to be appreciated for their excellent presentation and interaction skills. They know how not to hurt people's feelings and give happiness in one way.

Action Required:

The qualities of honesty and truth have to be practiced and you need to understand the law of karma so that intentions can become pure.

Category 3:

The souls have both impure intention and negative presentation.

Example: You dislike someone and you treat them in a mean manner. It is very easy to see such intention and behavior.

Action Required:

They have a lot of work to change both their intention and behavior. Thought pattern, belief system and attitude have to be modified and cautious effort is required in transforming the presentation manner. Self-reflection and deep shift has to be happen within.

Category 4:

This is the divine category where both the intention and presentation is benevolent. The eyes of such souls sparkle with truth and purity. Their behavior is kind, sweet and royal.

They are transparent. They take great care of people's feelings and express clearly their thoughts. Everyone feels safe in their presence. People seek their company. They always give love and happiness in a very natural way.

Action Required:

They have to harmonize their intentions and behavior. The inner world and external world has to be aligned. The heart should open up and embrace its full potential to see one's own beauty and the beauty of others. Meditation is a good pathway to begin this process. Each of us falls naturally in a category above and may also move between categories for certain actions.

Whatever category we are in, the fourth category is what God is teaching us to develop in our lives.

Reflection:
1. Does my intentions match my behavior? Let me write some situations where they didn't match.
2. Today let me see someone's intention behind their negative reaction.
3. Can I improve my presentation skills? Let me write three skills I need.

Om Shanti (I am peace)

The Journey from Guilt towards Forgiveness

We feel guilty not while making mistakes but when we realize those mistakes.

Mistakes are made in two ways.
1. One is not aware that it is a mistake, he/she thinks it is right but it turns out to be a mistake. Guilt in this case is minor and can be easily recovered. Some may not even feel guilty in such occurrences.
2. One is aware that it is wrong but still proceeds to make that action knowing the consequences. Guilt in this case is major and takes time to recover.

The Birth of Guilt:
Whenever the conscience and intuition is killed in the fighting process between mind and intellect, guilt occurs.
Example 1: Say you get a strong intuition in your mind that you need to take an umbrella, but the intellect becomes careless and skips that idea, and if it rains, you feel guilty.

Example 2: You desire to buy a camera. In the selection process, the conscience tells you that the camera's technical specifications are not good enough but because of your liking for the camera you get it. Later if the camera gives you issues, your conscience bites and you feel guilty.

Guilt not only occurs with the result of actions but also with our thinking, perceptions, belief systems about a person/

object/situation. Sometimes we say: "I am sorry for thinking wrong about you. I misunderstood you and misjudged the situation and behaved in a wrong manner."

Guilt is an emotion disempowering the soul and makes the self feel incapable and inferior. Guilt leads to inferior complexity. It destroys the courage and compassion of the soul.

Why guilt is not healed?
We all feel guilty but we have to transform that guilt into realization and forgiveness. Some of them feel guilty for their certain actions for many years and even their entire lifetime. The reason for the long time guilt is they are unable to,
- Accept
- Let go
- Forgive the self

They punish themselves by playing their mistakes again and again in their mind and feel bad for their misjudgment, unkindness or any weakness. They also ignore the people involved in their guilt.

Way to Freedom:
The guilt in relationships can be resolved by open communication, honesty and bigheartedness.

Accepting one's wrong behavior/mistake/weakness is the first process of any healing process.

Letting go of events, time, memories and your own past is essential to move on. Things happen for us to learn. Like a swan, I pick up the jewels of goodness in life and skip the stones of bad events. It is said the most difficult person to get forgiveness from is your own being.

Forgiving the Self:
- Realize the mistake
- Accept
- Learn
- Embrace
- Move on
- Offer a chance

Forgiveness is like erasing the writing board for our new lessons. Cheering the self up and giving hope for the future.

I need to love and teach my own inner child for it to laugh, smile, learn, play and enjoy the game of life daily.

Why should I forgive someone?
So that I could be light, free and happy. I also need to not hold any grudges inside me. My heart will be cool and healthy. If I hold onto something that keeps on pricking me, I am the first person to suffer.

How can I forgive?
When I totally take my thinking away from the person's identity/image I have created in my mind.
Example: He/She should behave like this or in a certain way.

Forgiveness is letting go of the expectations, disappointments of people I have created in my mind. To lower my bar of expectation and provide more room for others to play their part.

The mistakes of others could be,

- Their behavior
- Words they spoke
- Facial reactions they have given

I have recorded them in my mind, and that is the reason I cannot forgive them because each time this past recording is triggered by a present action, it brings the same emotional pain it had caused me in the past. I store and hold onto the memories that occurred many years ago like childhood experiences. I am unable to let go of them then I am stuck.

Therefore along with forgiving, I also need to forget, i.e., to erase the memory (images, words, action, loss, and pain) associated with that pain. Being a master creator, I can create my memories. Then I also have the power to delete the entire negative and waste memories I have created by becoming a master destroyer.

I can forgive someone only when I temporarily remove him or her completely from his or her role and relationship they are in with me.
Example: Say my brother insulted me, I can forgive him only when I remove my identity/recognition of him from the role "brother" he is playing.

I should temporarily disconnect him from that space of "brother" and see him just as a soul who is subject to mistakes/errors/bad moods/faults. In simple words, detach the script from the actor and seeing only the actor, I can be in a better place to understand and forgive that person.

I bring myself into this understanding that my brother is not perfect and might have misunderstood me or is not in a right state of mind (taking in a positive spotlight of whatever happened).

I should not judge a person based on their behavior/action/ words. I might have missed their good intention and where they are coming from based on my attitude, mood and situation. This awareness helps me to forgive and forget considering bitter scenes as side scenes of a trip and move ahead with absolute lightness and easiness.
I live as a cool and free soul.

Om Shanti (I am peace)

Letting Go and Moving On

Letting Go is an art of living in the present moment, keeping past to be past and allowing future to happen in its own time.

Qualities required for Letting Go:
1. Openness
2. Acceptance
3. Flexibility (power to adapt and mold)
4. Ever ready
5. Lover of Cleanliness

I can let go of something only when I am prepared to adapt and be open for new happenings in life.

When I don't Let Go:
1. Accumulation
2. Occupies space in my heart as bitter memories
3. I become heavy

When lots of data gets stored repeatedly, it leads to "Memory full" in my phone. Likewise my inner storage becomes overloaded with too much thinking and emotions. The sign of it is heaviness in my heart and I feel miserable.

4. Impurity — waste and negative thoughts
5. Confusion in the intellect (no clarity)

The memories of people's behavior, hurts, scars and situations create plenty of waste thoughts in me by constantly questioning their existence and occurrence in my life.

As I question, I am unable to find an answer.
I get confused and gradually negative thoughts of betrayal, jealousy, ego, anger, frustration, and anxiety arise.

How can I let go?
In cricket, a batsman keeps on hitting every ball that comes towards him. Even if he couldn't take any run in one ball, he continues to play and moves on to the next ball. If he stops and keeps thinking about his previous performance and become emotional, he cannot give his best shot for the next ball. Similarly I need to develop an attitude to keep progressing in my life.

Nothing should hold me behind that I get stuck. I can stop and look back only to cherish the good and capture the lessons I have learnt from my past.

Everything happens for a reason. Even bitter experiences has a purpose. I develop acceptance and openness to embrace whatever life is going to bring.

Good or bad, know there is always a lesson and hidden benefit in everything. Due to fear of people's opinion, I may think it's abnormal if I do not hold on. I may be judged by others as aloof and uncaring. But the true nature of our being is to be free at every moment. From this freedom, true love and care originates.

Since childhood, all of us get conditioned to capture and hold on. Spirituality reminds us to let go of external matters and connect to our innate nature of freedom. I can be free from my emotions as it is my own creation!

Practice:
Every one hour I remind myself:
- Today I make a determined thought to keep a full stop to whatever happens and I am ready for the next moment...

- Today I will completely accept whatever comes to me... I am completely prepared and ever ready for my day...

- When anything pushes me to be rigid and when I am about to enter the web of thoughts, I pause and remind myself 'I am a free soul, nothing can jail me.'

- I take a deep breath in. As I breathe out, I let go of all the emotions and become light.

Om Shanti (I am peace)

Techniques of Letting Go

Letting Go is a beautiful process where you allow yourself to become light and create space inside your heart. You let go of the old stuff that occupied your heart and let new things to come in.

Letting Go is an invitation for newness and new energy to fill in.

What to let go?
- Past bitter memory/experience.
- Person that hurt/betray/harmed you in any way or you believe he/she did that to you.
- Place – the events of that place you got involved in.
- Situation – unable to accept the way things occurred to you.
- Loss of a loved one/object.
- Bitter breakups and turmoil in relationships, e.g., a dispute within your family members.
- Your creative project, e.g., your project didn't turn out the way you wanted, your potential/talent wasn't recognized.

Techniques of Letting Go Process:
Technique 1 "Tree of Attachments"
Take a paper and pen. Draw a simple tree with four branches. See yourself as the bird sitting on a branch of this tree. Name the branches as the areas of attachment in your life. The leaves in the tree represent the attachments in that particular area.

Example: You can name one branch as "work" and the leaf could be "irritation with my boss." The other leaves could be "expecting a raise" or "cold war with a colleague."

Once you have placed your attachments on the tree diagram, you will get a visual of what you are going to work on. The visual energy helps both the subconscious and conscious mind to dissolve the strings that has been created. You can visualize yourself as a "bird" that is holding the branch tightly. You are unable to let go as you want something from that person/situation so badly that you are caught up in this expectation.

Example: "They have to change then I can change," "They have to apologize to me," and "They are so mean, I am so good to them."

All these expectations are your thoughts and gives you a reason to hold on to the present behavior of yourself towards that person/situation.

Example: You find yourself avoiding a person who talked behind your back. Each time they come to you, you feel uncomfortable and a memory flashes justifying you to avoid eye contact or move away.

Your Behavior: Avoidance

Your Justification: "They were so mean to talk behind my back."

Your expectation: "That is so not right. How could they do this to me?"

Feeling: Hurt and disrespect.

What I have to let go here?
I have to let go that branch of my expectation.
Some of our common expectations are:
Everyone has to be nice to me and not mean.
Everyone should love me and not gossip about me!
Everyone should respect me and not insult me!
These are some of the thought patterns we have created and we hold on to this expectation. We depend our feelings on those expectations and we find it hard to change them.
Instead of changing our self, we force others to change their behavior according to us.

Technique 2 "Our inner formula for feelings/emotions"
We have created numerous formulas inside us since our childhood and keep creating them as we experience life.

Formula for Happiness:
Person+ Response == Expectation - Happiness
When the person's response matches my expectation, I am happy.

Formula for Sadness:
Person+ Response xxx Expectation - Sadness/Hurt
When the person's response mismatches my expectation, I am hurt.

Relationship Formulas:
Say I have an expectation that my spouse should be
understanding.

Spouse+ Understanding == Expectation - Love
When my spouse is understanding which matches my
expectation, I feel love.

Spouse+ Conflict xxx Expectation - Dislike/Anger
When my spouse and I disagree which mismatches my
expectation, I feel dislike/irritated.

Boss+ Appreciation == Expectation - Feeling great
When my boss appreciates me which matches my expectation,
I feel great.

Boss+ Correction xxx Expectation - Awful
When my boss corrects me which mismatches my expectation,
I feel awful.

Situation + Result == what I want - Happiness

Situation + Result xxx what I want - Grief/Sad/Worry
A situation turns out to be as I expected(what I want), I am
happy and if not, I worry.

We all have inner formulas for our feelings and thereby
behaviors. There is an inner reasoning. When the inner
formula matches (green signal), you easily create positive

feelings. When it doesn't match (red signal), you create negative emotions.

Homework:
Discover your inner formulas.
- Choose important relationships in your life and write your formulas.
- Write your expectations from that relationship and the current state of that relationship. Do the matching and observe your corresponding feelings.

You will come to know a lot about your inner world!
Most of us usually blame one part of the formula and break our heads to fix that formula to work for us. That is how I am conditioned to force people to change and make my formula work.
Example: In this below formula,

Teenager + Behavior === Listen - In control (parent)

Teenager + Behavior xxx Listen - Frustration (parent)

When your teenager kid doesn't listen to you, you try to blame one part of the formula that my son/daughter doesn't listen to me and you get frustrated/worried about it. You make all effort to change your son/daughter's behavior and become further upset when it doesn't work.

But spirituality inspires us to change the other parts of the formula and also enables you to change the formula itself!

You are the creator of the formula! You can use your wisdom and experience to design a new formula that works irrespective of the external environment. That is the power of self-realization and the magic of the inner world. You will feel such deep inner power inside you that nothing can touch you.

The other part of the formula are "listen" and the feelings created through it. Instead of expecting that certain behavior from your teenager, you can change your inner formula to give you peace of mind and still have patience to work with him/her.

Designing a new formula for a teenager:
Teenager + Behavior (listen) === Openness - Feeling okay (parent)

Teenager + Behavior (not listen) xxx Openness - Feeling okay (parent)

In the above formula, you program your mind that instead of expecting "Listening" output from your teenager kid, you are going to be open with his/her behavior. If he/she listens to me, that's okay. If he/she doesn't listen to me, that is also okay.

Here you make an effort to change your expectation/programming to openness/tolerance/understanding so that you could be peaceful inside. When you are open, you can listen more. When you have a fixed expectation, listening and understanding stops.

Technique 3 "Meditation on Freedom"

Layers of Dependencies and Strings:

When we were born on this earth, each one of us naturally gets woven with the layers of strings and dependencies of this world. The layers of the body, relationships, work, material possessions and environment keep us tied up in the material world and sometimes not allow us to access the real self and the inner treasures merged within it.

As we grow up, we learn to derive peace, love, happiness and all sorts of human needs from these layers. Gradually we let the outside layers control our inner world. The inner world consists of my consciousness, thoughts, feelings, decisions, intuition, beliefs, perceptions and memories. The subtle invisible energy is within this inner world that expresses itself in the outside world through the layers.

Example: When my inner consciousness is of love then as a loving being, I think lovingly, I feel love, I see love, I record loving memories, I make loving decisions and ultimately manifest love in action through my body, relationships, objects and environment.

Meditation:
- How to connect with your inner being?
- How to find your real self?
- How to access your inner core?
- How to tap into your inner potential?
- How to be centered?
- What is mindfulness?

All the above questions have the same answer: "Meditation." Peel down each layer one by one. Go deeper and deeper until you reach your inner core.

Guided Meditation to touch the inner core and feel your real self:

Relax your body... feel your breath... breathe in and out...

Let go of the environmental layer:

- I gently let go of my environment layer... I go beyond my surroundings, noises and the place I live...

- I am free...

Now I move on to the next layer of work:

- I let go of all my worries, responsibilities, and the role I play in my life...

- Nothing is mine... I let go...

- I am free...

Moving on to the next layer of material objects and possessions:

- I let go of all the things I use in my life...they are given to me for a reason and temporary use...

- They are not mine... I let go...

- I am free...

Moving on to the next layer of relationships:

- I let go of all the people I know in my life... I let go of all my loved ones... I let go of everyone that surround me...

- I fly beyond as if I am a free bird... I accept them but I let go as of now...

- I am free...

Moving on to the next layer of body:
- I let go of the awareness of my body... each part in the body... each cell in the body...

- I am free... they are not mine...the body is my vehicle.

- I am separate from my body...

- I just use my body to express myself...

- I am free...

Being at the core:
- I have no layers around me...

- I am so light... I am centered... I see my being... I see my light... this is me...

- The real Me... pure light... pure love... just peace... I am peace...

- I am at my core... complete light, peace and acceptance...

- I feel myself...

Om shanti(I am peace)

Reflection at the end of the year and Letting Go

I scroll the pages of this year and see,

- What did I learn this year?
- What did the best experiences of this year give me?
- What did I accomplish both materialistically and spiritually in this year?
- Did I make any mistake? Can I forgive myself now and clear my slate?
- How were my relationships this year? - quality of interaction, sharing of love, happiness, harmony, adjustment level, tolerance level?

Answer these questions honestly in a piece of paper or your diary. Now no matter what answers you get, you have the choice of practicing the art of letting go.

What I have to let go?

- bad or bothering incidents/memories in this year
- mistakes of yours and others
- anything past of previous years
- worry about future
- fear of losing something
- current problems
- conflict and difference of opinion

Letting Go of Past:

Say you are holding a pen in your hand. Is the pen holding you or you are holding the pen? You! Right? Similarly, in life things come and go, the challenge/situation/problem goes away but I do not let go of them in my mind. I hold on to it for the rest of my life and I get stuck.

When I am stuck, there is no energy flow, i.e., I don't experience love, happiness and peace in my life constantly.

Even if I do experience them when my heart opens and the intellect momentarily forgets, they stay only temporarily. After some time, I go back to my habitual complaining/guilt/blame mode that make my peace and happiness vanish.

Letting Go in Relationships:
In relationships, sometimes it is very vital to sacrifice and compromise. It may be ideas, opinions, comfort zone, likes/dislikes, goals and habits.

Why I need to sacrifice or let go of them?
When I understand that by letting go of my idea or opinion, I can win their heart. I can gain their love, support, cooperation, contentment and respect which is far better than being adamant. By making little sacrifices of what I want in certain situation I can bring harmony in my relationships.

Letting Go of Materialistic Damage/Loss:
I didn't bring anything when I came to this world and neither can I take anything materialistic when I return home. So what is there to lose? Anything I lost was for the body and not for

the soul. The strengths of the soul are positive virtues, powers, good personality and good karma. With these powers, I can construct and create a new world around me. The pure soul power attracts the material needs of the body. The law of attraction works on purity.

Letting Go of Mistakes:
I have to understand that nothing and no one is perfect in this world. In winter season, we do not expect hot weather rather we prepare ourselves accordingly. Likewise in this world where each soul's battery is weak, all are bound to make mistakes. Each soul is a seeker of peace and love.

Let me become an image of forgiveness, mercy and understanding and take things in the lighter vein and cooperate with each other. After all we are flowers of the same garden. Aren't we?

Om Shanti(I am peace)

Which Spiritual Hero/Heroine You Are?

Heroes and Heroines play a key role in a movie. Movies are just a reflection of reality. In life, a real hero is the one who always stands for every one's benefit and makes his life valuable by supporting others' needs.

A hero/heroine never gives up; he/she finds happiness in the happiness of others. They take good care of the self, body and mind along with caring for others. They maintain balance in life. They become merciful when the weaknesses of others erupt; they never react or fight with them. They know each one's specialty and move along accordingly. Their heart is open and generous leaving no room for expectations.

Their thoughts, words and actions are always aligned. You will never find a hero/heroine gossiping about others. They always support the one who is harassed. Are you such a hero/heroine? There are eight categories of heroes/heroines described here. Choose who you are!

1. Hero/Heroine of Spiritual Knowledge:

Your base is Spiritual Knowledge, Wisdom, and Learning. You will run life based on your experiences, wise decisions and apply spiritual knowledge at every scene of your life.

You are very wise that you know the secret of every personality, action and situation. You always see the three aspects of time (past, present and future) knowing the beginning, middle and end of every situation that rises and ends. You never wander in the past and future but stay in the present moment. You stay stable and mature in your seat of farsightedness and wisdom.

You always stay as a guide to others enlightening each individual with simple solutions. You are always curious to learn and develop your spirituality and spiritual wisdom.

Your power: Power of Intellect.

2. Hero/Heroine of Spiritual Wealth:
Your base is Spiritual Wealth, Abundance and Prosperity.
You use your accumulated treasures of,
- Spiritual knowledge
- Your qualities and powers

As you are abundant, you can't help yourself from giving, sharing and distributing.

You always fill the hearts of many. Others feel prosperous in your company. Wherever you are, there is an atmosphere of abundance, fullness and prosperity. Everything flourishes in your presence. You are full of abundance.
Your power: Generosity and Kindness.

3. Hero/Heroine of Benevolence:
Your base is Goodness, Benevolence and Magic (Transformation power).

You always find some benefit/positive/goodness in any person or situation. You perform the magic of changing negative into positive, wrong into right and waste into useful. Wherever you are; there is magic and only solutions. Your eyes only see the light and darkness isn't visible to you even though it's there. Your power: Benevolent vision and attitude.

4. Hero/Heroine of Coolness:

Your base is Coolness, Calmness and Freedom.

You deal with everything in life with total ease under 'Take it Easy' policy along with responsibility. Nothing can push your button since you act from the space of self-mastery. You are free at heart and there is no wave of tension or worry visible in your face. You are a hero/heroine who extinguishes the fire of anger and any sort of negativity.

When you walk amidst a gathering, an atmosphere of coolness, easiness and calmness prevails.
Your power: Aura of coolness.

5. Hero/Heroine of Contentment:

Your base is Contentment and Gratitude.

You move along in your life with the support of contentment. You are content with everything and anything. You appreciate all the beauty and fortune that life has given you and with this power you easily make others content.

No one can blame or complain about you since you are content any way and fly beyond all ordinary matters.

You always stay in the beautiful cloud of contentment where life, people and situations are just like a cartoon show, which you enjoy watching. In your company distressed and disappointed hearts get colored by your contentment in seconds.

Your power: State of fulfillment and Pleasant smile.

6. Hero/Heroine of Fearlessness:

Your base is Courage and Bravery.

Nothing can make you afraid. You never run away from obstacles. You move mountains and cross seas (in terms of the amount) to achieve your goal.

You are deterministic and persistent. You always wear the armor of bravery and use the sword of inner power. People get inspired in your presence. You take initiatives, give a voice and work for greater cause. Everyone is protected under your strong umbrella of courage. You make weak into strong (like making a tiny leaf into a sword) with your powerful words and behavior.

Your power: Strength and Will power.

7. Hero/Heroine of Sustenance:

Your base is Nurturing, Love and Sustenance.

You move along on the basis of love and care. You care for every being in this world including nature and animals. With your gracious eyes; you always give a sense of belonging to anyone who comes into your contact.

Your heart always beats for love, care and sustenance. The world is nurtured from your pure and unconditional heart. You forgive and forget all the bad; giving only pure feelings of love and compassion.

Your power: Unconditional Heart.

8. Hero/Heroine of Zeal and Enthusiasm:

Your base is Happiness, Joy and Hope.

Your very spirit is filled with zeal and enthusiasm. Bells of joy and happiness ring in your presence. You elevate people's hopes and show them the path to happiness. Nothing can upset you or put you off mood. You color moody faces into delightful faces and enable all to celebrate life and goodness still in it. You lighten the lamps of hope in hopeless minds and creativity pops in with its new ideas and opportunities.

Your power: Rainbow colors of happiness.

Remember there is a hero/heroine inside each of us; perhaps I have it all!

Reflection:

- Choose a hero/heroine each week and practice being it. Observe the difference in you.
- Identity which hero/heroine others are. Share your experiences with them.

Om Shanti (I am peace)

About the Author

Padmapriya Mahendarkar Alias Sister Priya is the Meditation Center Coordinator of the Brahma Kumaris, St. Louis branch and a Raja Yoga meditation practitioner since 2002.

She has Bachelors in Information Science and Masters of Business Administration and has worked in the Telecom industry at India for eight years. At 2009, she dedicated her life with the Brahma Kumaris and became a full fledged Raja Yoga teacher in USA.

Since then she has been facilitating self development classes and workshops for people from all walks of life. Her classes are simple, engaging and motivational. Her guided meditation commentaries are soothing and provides deep experiences to the listener.

Sister Priya is also the author of "100 Inspirational Thoughts Part 1" book.

For any questions on the book, feel free to email at bksisterpriya@gmail.com

About the Brahma Kumaris

The Brahma Kumaris World Spiritual Organization acknowledges the intrinsic goodness of all people. They teach a practical method of meditation that helps individuals understand their inner strengths and values.

A worldwide family of individuals from all walks of life, they are committed to spiritual growth and personal transformation, believing it to be essential in creating a peaceful and just world.

The Brahma Kumaris World Spiritual University in Mt. Abu, India, is an international non–governmental organization (NGO) in general consultative status with the Economic and Social Council of the United Nations and in consultative status with UNICEF. It is also affiliated to the UN Department of Public Information. Through its international network of centers, the BK's organize special activities, seminars, workshops, dialogues, conferences, and exhibitions to provide people with spaces to voice their opinions on critical matters that impact their daily lives.

Raja Yoga Meditation

The Raja Yoga Meditation taught by the Brahma Kumaris comprises the three following segments.

Relationship with the Self:
This session provides the BK Teachings on knowing the self, understanding and embracing the strengths and weaknesses of the self. To discover the inner beauty and experience the original virtues of the self. Once the self is understood it paves the way to easy transformation of negative into positive. This session also helps one to understand one's thought patterns, habits and nature.

Relationship with the Source:
This session provides the BK teachings on One Source, the ability and process to tap into the Universal Source of powers. To connect with God without religion but with a direct loving relationship. To experience the spiritual connection between the self and God and recharge the inner self.

Relationship with Karma:
This session provides the BK Teachings on the importance of time and actions. To understand the effect of every action in this world and how to align our thoughts, words and actions. To learn the deep philosophy of Karma and cultivate a natural way of giving happiness and taking happiness in our relationships.

To learn meditation:

To find your local BK center, go to www.us.brahmakumaris.org and look under "Locations."

9781737036005